CREATI
A
STAFF HANDBOOK

Clare Hogg, MIPD, is a consultant and writer specialising in human resources and marketing. As a consultant she covers a wide range of projects – competency frameworks, internal communication strategies, management development programmes – for a wide range of organisations, from major multinationals to small companies, across both the public and private sectors. As a journalist and writer she has written for all the quality press and professional magazines. She is co-author of the MBA-accepted text *Frontiers of Leadership* and currently edits the IPD Information Notes series. She is also an accredited company director.

The Institute of Personnel and Development is the leading publisher of books and reports for personnel and training professionals, students, and all those concerned with the effective management and development of people at work. For details of all our titles, please contact the Publishing Department:

tel 020-8263 3387

fax 020-8263 3850

e-mail publish@ipd.co.uk

The catalogue of all IPD titles can be viewed on the IPD website:

www.ipd.co.uk

CREATING A STAFF HANDBOOK

CLARE HOGG

INSTITUTE OF PERSONNEL AND DEVELOPMENT

Design and typesetting by
Wyvern 21, Bristol

Printed in Great Britain by the Short Run Press, Exeter

British Library Cataloguing-in-Publication Data
A catalogue record for this book is available
from the British Library

ISBN 0-85292-822-X

INSTITUTE OF PERSONNEL
AND DEVELOPMENT

IPD House, Camp Road, Wimbledon, London SW19 4UX
Tel.: 020-8971 9000   Fax: 020-8263 3333
Registered office as above. Registered Charity No. 1038333
A company limited by guarantee. Registered in England No. 2931892

Contents

Acknowledgements   vi

Introduction: Who is this book for and
what does it provide?   1

1   Staff handbooks   3

2   How to compile and produce a staff handbook   11

3   Implementing your policies and procedures   31

4   Content   37

5   Legal aspects   65

6   Marketing your staff handbook   69

Bibliography   81

Useful organisations   85

Appendices

1   *Example Policy – British Airways*   91

2   *Example Policy – Scope*   95

3   *Example Policy – BBC*   99

Acknowledgements

To my mother:

a walking, talking handbook for life

And to Sue Filmer, Jean Richards, Rachel Preston and
Stephen Hurley, friends in need indeed!

Other titles in the series

Bullying and Sexual Harassment
Tina Stephens

Drugs and Alcohol Policies
Tricia Jackson

Induction
Alan Fowler

Part-Time Workers
Anna Allan and Lucy Daniels

Smoking Policies
Tricia Jackson

Introduction: Who is this book for and what does it provide?

This book aims to help both those producing a staff handbook for the first time and those revising an existing publication. Most of the information will be useful to you whatever the size of your organisation. The more employees you have, the more complex your policies and procedures are likely to be, the larger your budget for the project, and the more people consulted, but those really are the main differences.

Almost inevitably, the process of writing or auditing a handbook results in the creation or revision of policies and procedures, so this book contains guidance not just on the practical logistics of creating the publication, but also on developing and assessing current practice.

Creating a staff handbook is an important project involving a lot of hard work. It's relatively easy to produce an unhelpful stuffy document that is stuck in a drawer and forgotten. This book is for those whose objective is to produce an informative document that everyone finds easy and enjoyable to use.

1

Staff handbooks

- ☑ Why are staff handbooks important?
- ☑ Definition
- ☑ How are they used today?
- ☑ What are the benefits?
- ☑ When is a staff handbook appropriate?

You are lucky! Your aim is to produce an informative document which everyone finds easy and enjoyable to use. Five years ago this would have been quite a challenge. Today, it's still a challenge, but new technology offers all kinds of possibilities. You may think corporate intranets are only for enormous multinationals. Not so. Anyone with a network, and a staff who almost without exception have easy, regular access to a linked computer, can have an on-line handbook which is quick and fun to use and easy to update. If you post your handbook on an intranet you can use colour, animated graphics, response forms and search facilities at very little cost and to very great effect.

Why are staff handbooks important?

The importance of an up-to-date staff handbook cannot be overemphasised. Employees need to know the rules of the environment in which they work. They need to know the basis and justification for these rules (policies) as well as what they and others are expected to do (procedures). And from a practical point of view, people need to know at a glance whether they have the current version, so the handbook must also be subject to a clearly marked review system.

Staff handbooks are important for employers and managers too. They provide the proof that employees are aware of the rules the organisation is asking them to uphold. Employees cannot be disciplined for breaking rules they never knew existed. Conversely, the handbook will also include information about the obligations accepted by the employer (the terms and conditions of employment). The staff handbook is therefore a fundamental tool to help managers run a business smoothly and efficiently.

Definition

The terms *handbook* and *manual* are used interchangeably, but the Oxford Dictionary defines a handbook as being 'a short manual or guidebook', and the word handbook does have a more accessible ring. *Handbooks* tend to cover general policies and outline procedures, and are rather more informal in style. *Manuals* are more likely to be heavy reference tomes containing detailed information of exactly what actions are required, often in order to comply with legal or

4

quality regulations. But both *handbooks* and *manuals* provide guidance and information.

At the very least, a staff handbook is an organised collection of policies and procedures. Usually it is more than that. Because they are often given to people who are new to the organisation, they normally also contain other information which attempts to put the organisation into context – a message of welcome from the chief executive or chairman, a short history, a mission statement, and so on. Staff handbooks can also contain information about amenities and services available.

How are they used today?

Staff handbooks are used in a number of ways: as a source of reference, in order to fulfil statutory requirements (described in Chapter 5), as a means of communicating, and as an aid to induction.

Handbooks offer an opportunity to make a clear statement of what is important to the organisation, of its culture and values. Handbooks can also be an enormous aid to induction (though not a substitute) because they provide consistent, clear information that a recruit can read at a time convenient to him or her.

In addition to staff handbooks, many organisations also produce manager handbooks, which are normally issued separately. (They may, for example, include information on conducting a disciplinary interview, or dealing with a poor sickness record.) Some also produce procedures for personnel staff which can either be incorporated within the text of manager handbooks or added as an appendix at the back. Alternatively, they can be produced as an entirely separate document.

What are the benefits?

The thorough research involved in the preparation of a staff handbook results in clearer employment practices. A little digging can reveal policies and procedures that are out of date, conflicting, unproductive, destructive to teamwork, unsupportive to the organisational culture, incomprehensible, and even downright unsafe!

Another advantage of having a staff handbook is that it allows contracts of employment to be kept to a reasonable length. Employers are now required to supply their staff with an enormous amount of information – which all becomes unwieldy unless properly managed – and the staff handbook is the ideal tool to simplify matters.

Most organisations introduce handbooks with the following benefits in mind:

- *consistency of dissemination.* A handbook provides a means of ensuring that every employee receives the same information in the same format.
- *alignment.* It often happens that personnel policies are developed on a one-off basis and are introduced sporadically. They are therefore not wholly consistent, and they do not always support each other. Producing a staff handbook often highlights discrepancies – sometimes policies in different divisions of a company are contradictory. A corporate handbook helps to provide cohesion between the different divisions and locations (within the UK or internationally) of an organisation. In other words, the handbook is a valuable tool for ensuring that everybody is 'singing from the same hymn-sheet'.

6

- *the facilitation of lateral moves.* This alignment enables lateral moves to be made more easily because the rules and arrangements are broadly similar across the organisation.
- *an increase in trust, an improvement in relationships.* A handbook helps to assure everyone that people will be treated equally. Inconsistent and discriminatory practices are reduced. The handbook will also support managers in enforcing corporate requirements and procedures, and help to minimise the potential for unhealthy disputes between managers and employees.
- *the devolution of the application of HR practices to managers.* More and more organisations are now producing a managers' handbook as a separate section or document. The idea is to give managers as much information and support as possible in order to enable them to operate in a self-sufficient way. It should also give guidance on when a situation ought to be referred to professional personnel staff. This is increasingly the motivation for producing such a document. The idea is to encourage managers to really manage (rather than use the personnel department as a prop to help deal with 'difficult' staff problems), so that the burden on the personnel department is reduced.
- *the reassurance of the staff as to the organisation's commitment to acting as a good employer.* A staff handbook will help to assure employees that the organisation intends to treat them reasonably and fairly. It is tangible evidence of the organisation's commitment to being a good employer.

& a consistency in all aspects of P.T.

- *improved industrial relations*. Clear policies and procedures also help to avoid industrial tribunal claims and improve industrial relations.

When is a staff handbook appropriate?

Staff handbooks are appropriate wherever there is a need to keep a collection of easily referenced policies and/or procedures. Even very small companies of only two or three people can find a staff handbook useful. It may simply be a file in which to keep the equal opportunities policy or the statement on quality – documents which a customer could ask for as part of a tendering process – together with documents relating to employment.

A small company or a company concentrated on one or two activities (for example, a telephone sales company in which most employees work in a call-centre) can often aggregate all its policies and procedures within a single handbook. Larger, more complex organisations may find it better to develop a whole series of handbooks aimed at different functions and/or levels of employee. In general, however, the fewer documents the better. One publication is easily and simply accessible to all.

An alternative approach is to produce two documents, the first containing only policies, and the second only procedures. Although this might seem to be a neater way of setting things out, and some people may find the two documents easier to write, it creates more work for readers. If, instead, you amalgamate the information within one document, it is easier for staff to use and prevents people from having to look in several different documents for information that could be contained in just one. The policy aspect corresponds to 'This is how we approach things here,' and the procedures aspect corrresponds to the logically following '. . . so this is what you are supposed to do about it.' It may seem obvious but it is amazing how many authors of employee handbooks forget that the main readership comprises employees, busy working people. The more difficult it is for them to find information, the less likely they are to bother, and the whole point of producing the handbook is thus negated from the start.

However, where complex procedures apply only to certain categories of employees (eg maternity considerations, company cars, pensions, relocation, etc) there are advantages to producing these as separate publications. And, of course, the larger and more complex the organisation, the more difficult it is to incorporate everything into one document.

Staff handbooks come in all shapes and sizes – your aim is to develop the format and content that is best suited to your organisation and its culture, that is most 'fit for purpose', and that is what the end users really want.

How to compile and produce a staff handbook

☑ The planning process
   Appoint those who are going to be involved – Develop a
   project plan
☑ Structure, layout and format
   Structure – Layout – Format
☑ Style
☑ Production
☑ Revision and maintenance

Information technology offers a whole new world to the staff handbook creator. Posting your handbook on your intranet opens the way to all kinds of advantages. By carrying out a simple search people can get the precise information they need without having to pore through indexes. It can be visually exciting – you can use image-figures who point or text that flashes on and off to get the attention of your audience. You can easily invite feedback, and quickly respond to it, introducing changes and revisions without delay. You can 'delight your customer' (eg the employee) by

11

linking forms and further information to text – everything they need is at their fingertips. Your handbook has become a valuable source of help and advice for everyone in your organisation.

The very first thing to do is to decide whether or not you are going to go down this route. Don't let the high-tech jargon put you off. Anyone with a network can post their handbook on an internal website. But beware! Writing and designing for the intranet *is* very different. Spend as long as you can 'surfing' the web. You will get lots of ideas and also begin to get the 'feel'. Long paragraphs look daunting. Your style must have more pizzazz. Forget the chairman when you write: think of your audience. Photographs take forever to download and often don't look effective. If at all possible, find a mentor – someone with experience who will make suggestions and comment constructively on anything you produce. There are some publications listed in the bibliography at the back of this book that give some useful tips. Also there is an example of how they do it at the BBC: notice that they've limited themselves to just six pastel colours – but to what effect! And this site takes no time to download.

Before getting wholly carried away, however, don't forget that the handbook often forms part of the contract of employment. Information must still be accurate and precise. And it must be easily accessible to everyone. This means that most organisations continue to find that they need to run intranet and hard-copy versions in parallel.

Before writing even a word of the new handbook, you need to develop a project plan, then make a lot of fundamental decisions about the format, style, and so on, and consider some of the logistics of the production process.

The planning process

No one should be under any misapprehension about the size and importance of such a project, which in a larger organisation could take up to a year to complete.

If the production of the handbook involves the development of new policies and procedures, and if it involves the use of a project team, the process will take considerably longer than it might otherwise do. Whether a project team is involved or not, if it is to be successfully conceived and introduced, the project will involve a certain amount of consultation. People will disagree or simply be negative about the whole exercise. Those involved in the production of a handbook have to be committed and energetic, and they must have their roles clearly delineated from the start.

Appoint those who are going to be involved

The first step in the planning process is to appoint those who are going to be involved. Consider the following:

- *senior management.* The concept for the project should come from board level – ideally from the chief executive, but also possibly from the personnel, the finance or the communications director or from the board collectively. However, the project also needs a champion to ensure progress, and this champion should be a 'heavyweight' individual who identifies enthusiastically with the project. He or she, except in very large companies, should also be at board level.
- *the chairman or the chief executive.* The chairman or chief executive should write an introductory

13

statement of welcome, and append his or her signature as approval of the handbook.

- *an individual with overall responsibility for the project.* In companies large enough to have a personnel function, the project should be managed by an individual from that function. This person may delegate sections to others within the function or outside it. See opposite for a list of useful skills and competencies for such a person.

- *an individual responsible for maintaining the handbook.* This may or may not be the individual responsible for creating the handbook. One person must be given the job of the collation and insertion of all new and revised information. If this is not done effectively, half the staff will be following obsolete regulations, and much of the benefit of having a staff handbook at all will be lost.

- *a project team.* As part of the consultative process and in order to ensure as much input from those who must implement the handbook, organisations sometimes use project teams. There are disadvantages to this. Inevitably, the use of a project team holds up the process. Also, if there is a serious disagreement about the approach or content, someone who has been a valuable ambassador for the handbook may metamorphose into a high-profile individual in violent opposition. When a project team is to be used, it is important to ensure that someone who is both a strong chairman and a skilled facilitator leads it.

Useful skills and competencies for those creating staff handbooks

'political' skills

The word 'political' is purposely written with a small 'p'. This person needs to be able to operate effectively at all levels of an organisation – senior management must respect him or her. Others (and their managers) must also be willing to help, support and co-operate, even if this person has no direct authority over them.

Meeting and presentation skills

The ability to chair and facilitate meetings is usually important, together with good presentation skills – for selling the handbook to senior management and running roadshows throughout the organisation.

Writing and editing skills

Obviously, this person must be able to write well – to set out information in a readable, logical and clear way. Very often some of the writing will have to be delegated to others. Then the co-ordinator must be able to edit their work.

Project management skills

Anyone responsible for creating a staff handbook has to be a 'completer/finisher' in Belbin's terminology – someone who gets things finished – because this sort of project can sometimes feel like walking through treacle. He or she must be able to divide the project up into digestible chunks and ensure that deadlines are met. He or she must in particular be well organised, so as to develop an effective filing system; otherwise, there will be paper and computer documents everywhere – finding things when they are needed will take forever, and so, therefore, will the whole process.

Managing the project team

1 If there is a trade union or other employee body, consider involving a representative from it. Make sure, though, that the person understands that he or she is there as an individual and not as a spokesperson. And take care that the group does not begin discussing union issues.

2 Consider asking managers to appoint employees to be part of this team, or asking for volunteers.

3 Depending on the length of the project, and how the different sections are handled, consider rotating membership to avoid people running out of 'oomph'.

4 Make it clear from the very beginning that the team's role is advisory. Recommendations are subject to approval by senior management.

5 Remember to issue agendas and follow up action points.

6 Remember to disband the team formally. It's a nice gesture to indicate the gratitude of the organisation through some form of celebration – buns at the coffee-break or drinks at a local pub – and express the thanks of the organisation clearly. Write to managers to thank them for allowing their direct reports to spend time on the project, and, if appropriate, praise the team member for his or her input.

- *support staff from other functions.* The project will need the help of staff from other functions. Obviously, there will be a need for helpful and patient administrative staff who will be asked to help with the production of endless drafts and redrafts. Staff in the IT, design and internal communications functions may also be involved, especially if you're posting this on the intranet. So may staff in the print-room if printing is to be done internally. Brief these people right from the outset and discuss their input and likely time commitment. You may think you know when and how to involve them – but how often is it that an expert whose advice is sought sighs sadly and comments, 'If only you had asked me this before . . .'? You will also need to gain the agreement at the outset of these people's bosses. Unless they support the involvement of their staff in your project, you will not get the help you need.

- *external consultants.* Especially if your company has no personnel function, or if there is no 'slack' in staff resources to allow the allocation of such a time-consuming (and often onerous) project, there is much to be said for using an external consultant. Make sure that the individual (or individuals) responsible for the project is both experienced and excellent at writing good copy. Ask for samples of his or her work, and check it particularly for user-friendliness – is it readable and clearly and logically set out?
- *a proofreader.* Someone with editing and proof-reading experience will be needed. This should not be the person who has written or typed the original document. Don't wait until the last minute to find this person. People with these skills are rarer than you might think, and tend to get booked up.

Develop a project plan

Once you have selected the people involved, you should work with them to develop the project plan and make sure that they buy into the plan and what they have undertaken to do. Think the plan through from first to last, and verify that the timings are realistic and will maintain the momentum. Be especially careful finally to think the plan through from the reverse direction. Try to organise concurrent development on independent sections because this will speed up the process and help to keep everybody motivated.

Stages of the project

1 Identify the need to develop a new handbook or revise an old one, including the research costs and resources required. Draw up a budget. Do you intend to post the handbook on your intranet? Are other documents – such as manager guidelines – also needed?

2 Gain senior management approval and commitment.

3 Identify those who will be involved, and gain their agreement and their manager's agreement for their role and input.

4 Work out a project plan (at the first project team meeting, if there is one) and gain everyone's commitment. Consider in particular:
- which policies/procedures are going to take the longest to develop or revise
- how to identify any new policies/procedures that may require piloting
- which policies/procedures can be developed concurrently and independently
- whether you need a 'quick fix' – to be able to show some

---

results early on – and if so, which policies/procedures are already in place and working well

● whether there are any policies/procedures for which people are urgently waiting.

5 Carry out internal market research.

6 Carry out an external benchmarking exercise.

7 Identify sources of information for the contents – eg from the IPD, the Industrial Society, the Equal Opportunities Commission (see the *Useful Organisations* section at the back of this book).

8 Agree:

● the presentation
● the layout
● the format
● the style
● the marketing plan
● the distribution
● the method of continuous revision and maintenance.

9 Buy in the necessary materials, equipment, software, reference books (see the bibliography and *Useful Organisations* sections at the back of this book).

10 Brief designers and illustrators, if any.

11 Consider practical ways to ensure that the new policies and procedures are implemented.

12 Begin writing the individual policies and procedures.

13 Pilot those that need to be piloted.

14 Ask those responsible for individual sections to check the draft of their sections.

15 Make the presentation to the management, and gain

approval either on a section-by-section basis or of the document as a whole (it depends on the structure, length and complexity of the draft, the organisational culture, and so on).

16 Get the document checked by a lawyer or legal department, either on a section-by-section basis or the document as a whole.

17 Get the document proofread by someone other than the person who has written and/or typed it in the first place, and preferably by someone with proofreading and editorial experience. Brief him or her carefully, telling him or her to look for clarity and readability as well as grammatical and typographical errors.

18 Send the copy to the designers, if any.

19 Organise the production of the document (or the individual section if you are issuing on a section-by-section basis):
- the printing
- the binding
- on disk
- on your intranet.

20 Begin your internal marketing campaign. You can do this before you distribute the document, but it is more usual to distribute the document as an integrated part of the campaign.

21 Distribute the document:
- as hard copies to each individual who should have one (ensure that employees sign for them if necessary)
- on the intranet.

22 Gain feedback.

23 Revise and maintain the contents.

Structure, layout and format

Your decisions regarding the structure, layout and format will depend largely on:

- your market research (see Chapter 6)
- your budget
- the structure, culture and size of your organisation.

Structure

Pay very close attention to the structure. This is absolutely key. A sloppy, illogical structure means that people won't be able to find their way around your handbook and it will therefore fail in one of its principal aims of being a handy reference document. It also means that you may miss things out in the compilation process.

It's a good idea to differentiate between contractual terms (the rules which should be obeyed, holiday and sickness provisions, the standards of dress code and time-keeping) and non-contractual terms (items which are not the contractual right of the employee – disciplinary and grievance procedures, the equal opportunities policy) by putting them in separate sections.

Develop a system (probably a numbering system: 1, 1.1, 1.1.1, or 1), 1a), 1a.i) for example) for identifying sections. Date each page or section so that you can check that an employee has the latest edition.

Decide whether you are going to separate policies and procedures or amalgamate them. Is any information going to be available as a separate document (eg pension scheme, maternity arrangements, etc)? Then consider how you are going to structure your text.

Short handbooks tend to cover each subject in just a couple of paragraphs. If you are producing a comprehensive manual, one common approach to presenting an individual policy is:

Section title and number
Date and page numbers (or 'page *a* of *n*' if it is a loose-leaf format)

1.1   The purpose/overall objective of the policy
1.2   Responsibility (who does the policy apply to, and what is their role in upholding it?)
1.3   The main features of the policy
1.4   Eligibility and conditions
1.5   Procedures.

Appendix 2: Scope at the back of this book gives an example of a manual that uses flowcharts.

If you are producing a managers' check-list, it is helpful to include boxes to tick. A document check-list for a manager who is having to deal with a case of bad behaviour might look something like this, for example:

Document check-list: Disciplinary interviews
Organisation's disciplinary policy and procedures
Note of the last time operational requirements were
   made clear to this employee
Timesheets
Complaints on file
Sickness/absence record
Notes of interviews with colleagues
Correspondence

Remember: *include only what is absolutely essential.*

Layout

Layout is also very important. If the budget affords it, a trained designer can make the document look much more professional, and does show the organisation's commitment to the handbook and to communicating effectively with employees in general. If you are producing the document on your personal computer, you may like to consider investing in some specialist software (see *Useful Organisations* at the back of the book). If you are going to get your handbook printed, speak to your printers before you buy in order to ensure that you choose software they can read.

Spend extra time and effort on the design of the cover. Avoid photographs that date easily.

If you are designing the layout yourself, there are a few helpful guidelines to follow. (If you are using designers, these guidelines may also be useful as an aid to assessing their work.)

1 Keep it *simple.*

- Limit the number of text groupings on each page. A simple test is to hold the page you're working on up to a mirror about five feet (nearly one and a half metres) away. Scan the page and count the number of times your eye stops. If it stops more than five times, reorganise your text.
- Use plenty of white space – don't cramp the page with text. In addition, use white space to help clarify relationships between text groupings and graphics on a page by displaying unrelated items further apart and related things closer together.

2 Keep it *consistent*.

- Consistency is particularly important in a staff handbook because it unifies a publication and enables readers to see at a glance how the information is organised.
- Make sure you are consistent in:
    spacing
    margin widths
    the space between each heading and its body text, or between pictures and their captions.
- Use fonts consistently. Text should be set in the same font throughout, except for headings, subheadings, captions and sidebars. Remember that fonts with serifs are much easier to read than sans-serif fonts (which is why they are the fonts that were used to teach us all how to read). Use serif fonts for body text, and sans-serif for headings and subheadings. Make sure you use a font of a reasonable size for the main text.

3 Use *contrast*.

- Contrast pulls the reader's eye to what's important. Try to ensure that there's one dominant element – big bold type or an interesting graphic – on each page or two-page spread. This helps to break the text up and make the page less daunting to look at.

4 Wherever possible use *graphics* – pictures, photographs, diagrams, graphs, drawings, etc. Flowcharts work particularly well for complicated procedures. See page 25 for guidelines on using flowcharts, the *Appendix 2: Scope*

example at the back of the book, or look at the 'Visio' website where there are some on-screen demonstrations.

- If you are using cartoons of people, consider using a gender-neutral figure whose sex cannot be identified.

Hints for creating flowcharts

Creating flowcharts

- Produce the draft-flowcharted overview of the whole procedure, breaking the flowcharts into small, natural segments.
- Use Post-It™ notes to work out the sequence of events.

General comments

- Keep the charts clean and uncluttered.
- Make the flow easy to follow, generally flowing from top to bottom.
- Use small amounts of text.
- Annotations should accompany text pages.
- Make sure each step is clearly described.

Use software to help

- 'Visio' is probably the most widely used flowcharting software (see *Useful Organisations* at the back of the book).

Format

Handbooks do not need to be overly glossy. But they should look professional.

There are a number of options to choose from:

- *loose-leaf or bound format.* There are many advantages to the loose-leaf format. It's easy to update (this means that in the long term it may also be the cheapest option), and it offers employees the facility to keep their own relevant documents conveniently together.

- *A4 or 'pocket' size.* There are enormous advantages to choosing the A4 size – above all, missing pages can easily be photocopied and new copies quickly printed out direct from a personal computer. There is a perception that 'pocket' size is more portable and more of a personal possession: in reality, staff handbooks are not things that people need to be able to carry around a lot.
- *colour-coding* for ease of reference.
- *with blank sheets at the back* for personal notes.
- *with a plastic folder* for holding supplements, etc. Terms and conditions that change frequently and/or vary between groups of employees – for example, pay, overtime or shift-working arrangements – can be issued as a supplement and kept at the back of the handbook.
- *with different textures, weights and crispness of papers.* Choose the paper very carefully. It is an integral part of the design of your handbook. Try printing out the same page on different papers, and compare.
- *with laminated sheets.* Some procedures can usefully be produced on an individual laminated sheet for specific situations. Banking and retail companies, for example, may keep brief, easy-to-read guidelines by tills outlining procedures in the event of an armed raid.
- *as posted on the organisation intranet.* I've already

26

explained that designing for the intranet is different from designing for the printed page. It's essential (well, very advisable) that your handbook is interactive. Enlist the help of your IT department and get a copy of Bryan Hopkins' excellent publication *How to Design and Post Information on a Corporate Intranet* (see the bibliography at the back of this book).

Remember also to practise what you preach. If you have clearly stated your organisation's commitment to environmental responsibility in your handbook, don't print on one side of the page only!

Style

In general a staff handbook should be written in a friendly, personalised, informal style, using 'we' and 'you' rather than 'the employee'. This helps a reader to relate more closely to the document. See page 28 for some further tips on better readability. For difficult and complex subjects, such as pensions or maternity, consider using a question-and-answer technique, putting forward points in the form of the sort of questions that are asked and giving the answers underneath.

Tips to improve readability

1   Never use a long word where a short (one- or two-syllable) word would do. Be straightforward. Use the language of everyday speech, not that of lawyers or bureaucrats (so prefer *let* to *permit*, *people* to *persons*, *buy* to *purchase*, *present* to *gift*, *colleague* to *peer*). Use the facilities of your computer software to edit your own documents – use the search function to spot words such as *permit* and *purchase*.

2   If it is possible to cut out a word, cut it out. Make every word work for you.

3   Never use the passive where you can use the active.

4   Never use a foreign phrase, a scientific or technical term or a piece of jargon if you can think of an everyday English equivalent. Especially avoid your own organisational jargon. Remember a very large part of your readership is new recruits.

5   Make sure your sentences stay short. Again, use the grammar-correction function of your word-processing software to help. This highlights long sentences and makes suggestions for cutting them down. Long paragraphs can also confuse a reader. A paragraph should be a unit of thought, not of length.

6   Write grammatically correct copy. If you have any doubts (particularly in relation to punctuation, which can be confusing) refer to *The Economist Style Guide*, or Martin Cutts' *Plain English Guide*, or, specifically for punctuation, to *Mind the Stop*. See the bibliography at the back of this book for details.

7   Be careful to be exact. For example: is the *day* you are mentioning a calendar day, a 24-hour period, or an eight-hour working day? Be very careful how you use *can*, *may*, *shall* and *will*. Steer clear of statements such as 'Your supervisor will always be willing to hear your complaint.'

8   Wherever possible, be positive rather than negative – use *do* rather than *don't*.

Production

At last! Having got all the copy approved and checked, and the layout finalised, now comes the time to publish the handbook. The easier and simpler you make it for the printer the better. Give very clear written instructions (including details of the disk format – eg Word™ – if applicable), and specify the quantity, the paper, the ink colour, double- or single-sided printing, the binding and/or other finishing, and the delivery date and place. Make sure everything is included and that it's obvious where any loose graphics should go. Check the proofs carefully, but try to avoid lots of minor corrections after the document has been typeset because they can be extremely costly.

Revision and maintenance

One person should be responsible for monitoring events and organisational changes that might necessitate amendments to the handbook. This is particularly important if the handbook is a document referred to in the employees' written terms and conditions of employment. It is equally important never to assume that an amendment to the staff handbook will happen automatically.

3

Implementing your policies and procedures

- ☑ Meetings
- ☑ Follow-up measures

Just about everyone can think back to government policies and civil service regulations that have been total disasters because they haven't been properly thought through. Organisational policies and procedures are no different. If you attempt to introduce an impractical policy or procedure, you are likely to be pilloried without mercy, and you will find it very difficult to get support for anything you do in the future.

This is why this chapter appears before the chapter on *Content*. Before beginning to write anything it is absolutely vital to consult and think through the process and the approach. Your policies and procedures must be reasonable, practical, and above all, necessary. The fewer rules and regulations you have, the fewer will be broken, and the less bureaucratic your organisation will appear.

This is where I have always found flowcharts to be enormously helpful. The first thing to do is to establish what is actually happening at the moment. Whether they are written or not, your organisation already has policies and procedures.

Meetings

For each subject area call a meeting of appropriate people. If, for example, you believe that the organisation's policy on x needs adapting to changed circumstances, you might invite A, B, C, and D to come and talk to you all together. Before the meeting, ask these people to write down a list of the questions that employees most often ask them on this subject, and a second list of the type of problems that they most often have to sort out which fall under this heading.

The agenda for this meeting is simple. First get a consensus about the current policy and its purpose. Then discuss whether this is still appropriate. If it isn't, review and improve it. Next draw a flowchart on the flipchart showing the step-by-step procedure for implementing the change. Allow quite a lot of time for this. Even in small companies it's amazing how people in one department can be completely unaware of the part played by those in another department. Revise the list of questions from employees and the list of typical problems. Then, again, discuss ways in which the procedure can be streamlined.

Make sure you've done your benchmarking on this subject (see Chapter 6) before the meeting, and that you have a fair idea what common practice and best practice are. Identify alternative approaches. You'll find it helpful to take examples of other organisations' policies and procedures to the meeting. Think through the current procedures. Arm yourself with every question you can think of on the subject. One immediate and very useful question to ask is simply 'Why?' Why do we do this? Why do we do it this way?

Your main role at this meeting is to gain as much good information as possible, so you should be endlessly asking questions. Remember to begin by:

- asking *open* questions (make no assumptions), eg 'So what do you do if you think an employee is guilty of a disciplinary offence?'

Then

- *probe* to find out more: 'How do you arrange the disciplinary interview?'

- ask *closed* questions to check details: 'Do you inform [him or her] of the date and location verbally or in writing?'

And finally

- use *checking* questions to ensure that your information is absolutely accurate: 'Did you say that the departmental secretary was responsible for generating this letter?'

If you are looking at a very complex, important, or groundbreaking policy and procedure (eg an appraisal system, or a mentoring system), it's a very good idea to pilot it first in a positively-minded department or division.

On the other hand, don't be afraid to simply axe a policy/procedure if you know it sounds good in theory but is wholly unworkable in practice. Policies on probationary periods and exit interviews are two which very often are simply not carried through. E-mail and internet policies are two more which are hard to police. If you are monitoring employees' e-mail and internet use, you should say so clearly.

Follow-up measures

Having made sure your policies are practical and reasonable, you then have to put in measures to see that they are adhered to. Your three most powerful tools are:

- training
- support
- inducements and deterrents.

If you can introduce your handbook as part of a training exercise, people will see the point of it, understand that it's of use to them, and therefore be more likely to use it. The training can be presented either as specifically linked to the handbook or as part of other training related to policies and procedures included in the handbook. It should be exciting, participative – and short.

People are also more likely to apply the more difficult policies and procedures if they know that help and support is at hand. This is particularly so in the case of disciplinary interviews, instances of bullying, alcoholism, and so on, in the face of which many managers feel out of their depth. Make it clear that the organisation encourages managers to seek additional help in these situations, and make it easy for them to get it – give a contact name and number.

Build in inducements and deterrents wherever possible. For example, make promotions to managerial positions subject to successful completion of appraisal training, and/or make it clear that any breach of an important procedure – such as ethics – will be dealt with as a disciplinary offence.

However you do it, don't let your policies and procedures become purely academic. They need to really *happen*!

Content

☑ Relating directly to the contract of employment	☑ Information technology
☑ Induction	☑ Equal opportunities
☑ Ethics	☑ Personal liability
☑ Authorities	☑ Health and safety at work
☑ Leave	☑ Employee communications
☑ Employment outside the company	☑ Personal records
☑ Leaving the organisation	☑ Employment of relatives or people with whom there are close personal ties
☑ Disciplinary and grievance procedures	
☑ Remuneration and benefits	☑ Employee voice
☑ Travelling on business	☑ Social
☑ Career development	☑ Support of charities
☑ Intellectual property	☑ Dress code or uniforms

This chapter constitutes a check-list together with guidelines, items to consider, and suggested approaches in relation to the content of a staff handbook. It is not intended to represent a 'model' handbook. Taking a 'standard' handbook and 'doctoring' it here and there is like buying a pair of ill-fitting shoes and trying to wear them in! It is much better to start with a clean sheet of paper. On the other hand, if you already have a number of well-written policies and procedures which are working well, or a friendly organisation in a similar industry has lent you a copy of its handbook, don't try to reinvent the wheel.

Pay a lot of attention to getting the title and the front cover right. First impressions count.

The handbook normally will begin with:

- a contents page – a basic organisational tool
- an introduction – this works well as a statement of welcome signed by the chief executive or chairman. The introduction should outline what the handbook is intended to do. This is the place to make it clear that the provisions and statements outlined in the handbook are not optional, and also that the organisation reserves the right to make changes using established procedures.

The introduction is then followed by some information about the organisation that may include:

- the mission statement
- the organisation's logo and its name and address
- a brief history
- its values and standards
- basic information about the field or business area in which the organisation operates, its turnover, where it ranks in industry league tables, how it is structured (where the different divisions are located) and recent major achievements
- an organisation chart (the flowcharting software 'Visio' – see *Useful Organisations* at the end of this

book – also includes an organisation chart facility)
- directors and senior management
- associated organisations.

Either at the beginning or at the end it is helpful to include:

- contact details for further information and to whom employees can give feedback
- details of where to obtain any forms referred to within the text
- blank sheets of paper for the individual's own notes
- an index, which is essential.

The main body of the handbook then covers a whole range of aspects of being employed at your organisation. The following is simply a check-list together with some points to consider. It would be most unusual to include *all* categories – but even this list is not exhaustive! Remember, the longer the document, the less likely people are to read it. Limit each topic to three paragraphs or a quarter to half a page.

As far as possible the handbook should aim to answer as many questions as possible and prevent time-consuming direct contact with various departments.

And of course remember that gender-neutral terms and titles should be used throughout.

Relating directly to the contract of employment

Contracts

Some organisations like to outline the different kinds of contract which different staff may be on – short-term, long-term, casual work and self-employed, full-time, part-time, shift-work, etc.

Probationary periods

Bear in mind that, legally, probationary employees have rights very similar to those of normal employees in most situations. They can, for example, claim unlawful discrimination on the grounds of sex, race or disability. Nevertheless, it's still a good idea to make it clear that new employees are subject to a probationary period. The employee is then put on notice that his or her performance is being carefully monitored. It may then also be taken into account by employment tribunals in deciding the fairness of any dismissal during or at the end of a probationary period.

In addition, your organisation may wish to offer reduced terms and conditions to probationary employees – for example, by not allowing the accrual or taking of holiday entitlement during the probationary period (subject to rights under the Working Time Regulations 1998). It is also possible to specify that during the first month of the probationary period the organisation, as the employer, may terminate the employment without formal notice or with notice of less than one week. It's only worth having a trial or probationary period, however, if there are effective structures within the organisation to make sure that the monitoring of new recruits really happens. Details of probationary periods are usually included in the contract or letter of appointment.

Notice periods

Notice periods are usually specified in the offer letter. It is not necessary to state that where an employee has been dismissed for gross misconduct, rights to notice from the employer are forfeited, but many handbooks do, for clarity.

Liability to transfer

Some employers include 'mobility' clauses in their contracts which require employees to move and work in different locations, either within the UK or internationally. Be aware that it's not always easy (or advisable) to enforce these clauses.

Conditions of service, including hours

This clause covers hours of work (including, where appropriate, lunch hours and breaks) and annual leave entitlement. You could include also flexi-hours, working from home, job-sharing, etc (see Flexible working on page 47).

Induction

The purpose of induction is to help people to settle in and become effective as quickly as possible. The *Good Practice Guide* (see the bibliography) on *Induction* covers this in full.

Ethics

Ethics is a matter of attitude more than procedure. Consider carefully how much detail you want to include. It should be just enough to:

- give support to employees – enabling them to say 'I'm sorry, I'm not allowed to accept that under organisation rules'
- make it absolutely clear what constitutes

unethical behaviour, and that it will not be
tolerated
- outline the very serious steps that will be taken in
the event of proven unethical behaviour.

Business gifts

The simple rule is to advise staff not to accept gifts. However, that is not always practical, and unfortunately, what
is 'normal' in, for example, the financial services sector
would be unacceptably profligate in, for example, the civil
service. One helpful guideline in judging whether a gift is
'appropriate' or not is to consider who is giving it (is it someone who could benefit from decisions made by the recipi-
ent?) and the timing of the gift (eg at the point of tendering,
or as a thank-you at the end of a job). Wherever there is the
possibility of doubt, employees should consult a senior officer of the organisation.

Disclosure of information

The staff handbook should clearly state that no employee
should disclose any confidential information to anyone outside, either while employed or after having left the organisation.

Security

Employees have a duty of care to safeguard the property
and equipment of the employer. Security regulations and
arrangements should be outlined and strictly adhered to.

Conflicts of interest

Employees should not allow their private interests to conflict with, or appear to be in conflict with, the interests of

the employer. Some organisations specify that corporate funds and facilities may not be used to support political parties.

Competition

This is put particularly well in Esso's *Standards of Business Conduct* in which it is stated that 'We will not tolerate an employee who achieves results at the cost of breaking laws or unscrupulous dealing. By the same token, we will support, and we expect our managers to support, an employee who passes up an opportunity or advantage which would sacrifice ethical standards.'

Authorities

Financial

No one without explicit authority to spend money should do so. In a medium to large organisation this authority is usually set down in writing and specifies precisely how much the individual is authorised to spend and for what type of transaction.

Speaking on behalf of the company

This is a good place to make it absolutely clear that if they are contacted by a representative of the media, employees should not make any statement and are not authorised to speak on behalf of the organisation.

Leave

Annual leave

Set out clearly the entitlement to paid holiday.

- It includes all public and statutory holidays (or the entitlement to pay for working on these days).
- It should state the number of working days per full calendar year, and when the 'leave year' begins and ends – usually 1 January and 31 December – and what this represents on a pro-rata monthly basis (eg '1.25 days for each completed month of service') for those joining or leaving part-way through the year.
- It is advisable to state that leave should be taken during the calendar year in which it is earned. To allow individuals to accrue leave can cause problems for other staff who may then have to stand in for them over long periods.
- Specify any additional days off over Christmas.
- Set out the system for booking leave. It is wise to state that all leave is subject to operational requirements and the necessity to maintain reasonable staffing levels.
- If you have a policy of allowing staff extra leave for years of service, set out the system here.
- If your organisation employs shift and part-time staff, explain how their leave entitlement is calculated.

Time off in lieu

If an employee regularly works long hours of unpaid overtime, is he or she entitled to take additional time off work?

Sick leave

State your organisation's policy in relation to sick leave. Most organisations require an employee to notify his or her manager on the first day of absence and as soon as possible – by noon at the latest. Absence for more than a certain number of days usually requires a doctor's certificate, which should specify a date for return to work if it is likely to be within 14 days. You may wish to specify a maximum number of days' leave for sickness within a period of 12 consecutive months, after which sick leave may be taken out of employees' annual leave.

You may wish to allow an employee who goes sick during a holiday period to set the days of sickness off against sick leave, so restoring days of holiday still to be taken. This may be subject to the presentation of a doctor's certificate and to an overall maximum number of days involved.

If your organisation has a policy on short-term disability leave, you may wish to include it here. This is also the place to include your organisation's policy in relation to medical and dental appointments, if it has one.

Some employers are registering pressure from employees to allow 'fertility leave'. This is leave taken in order to undergo medical treatment for infertility. Be aware that the amount of time required can be considerable and ongoing.

Special leave

This includes *compassionate* leave (eg on the death of a close relative) or *domestic* leave (eg for those with caring responsibilities). It can also cover *public duties* such as jury service, standing for Parliament or sitting as a Justice of the Peace. Leave allowance may also be made for those who belong to the reserve forces of the Armed Forces or the Special Constabulary. And it can cover time off for trade-union activities.

Unpaid leave

This is covered under other headings, such as Sabbaticals, see below.

Sabbaticals

More and more people are wanting to take significant chunks of time off for a whole variety of personal reasons – to care for children or relatives, to undertake full-time study, or simply to travel around the world. State your organisation's stance on this.

Maternity and paternity leave; also family and adoption leave

Maternity leave is rather complex – and in any case you may wish to cover it in a section of its own, together with maternity benefit.

A concise way of dealing with this subject within the handbook, however, is to state that once the pregnancy is confirmed, the personnel department (or if there is no personnel department, whoever is responsible for the payroll) should be informed in order then to provide details of the procedure.

Paternity leave and other types of leave can usually be covered fairly succinctly.

Flexible working

What flexible working arrangements does your organisation offer? Try specifying core time (eg 10–12, 2–4). Contact New Ways to Work (see *Useful Organisations* at the back of this book) or consult the *Good Practice Guide* on *Part-Time Workers* (see bibliography) for further information.

Employment outside the company

Moonlighting

You may wish to set out your organisation's policy in relation to employees who work part-time for other employers.

Non-executive directorships, governorships, etc

Many employers encourage employees to take on non-executive directorships, governorships, and so on, as a way of grooming them for director-level appointments within the organisation. State your organisation's policy on this, including any time restrictions, and (if there is no 'conflict of interest' clause) possibly add a proviso to the effect that 'Outside jobs, investments, or other activities that may lessen the impartiality of your judgement or interfere with your effectiveness or productivity must be avoided.'

Leaving the organisation

On leaving the organisation for whatever reason, employees should return all the organisation's property (eg mobile phones, documentation, computer equipment, etc). As further encouragement you may wish to state that a failure to do so may incur a deduction from any final payment due.

Exit interviews

State why these interviews are held – what is done with the information – and when and by whom (personnel department, line manager, etc) these interviews are conducted.

Resignation

State what the organisation's provisions are in the event of outstanding holiday entitlement (the organisation may not wish to make any reimbursement in the case of gross misconduct or where an individual has left without giving notice) or when more leave has been taken than the holiday entitlement.

Retirement

State clearly the normal retirement age and what provisions there are for early or late retirement. Identify any pre-retirement guidance given by the organisation.

Redundancy and redeployment

Some organisations prefer not to include information about redundancy, on the grounds that it seems unnecessarily negative and pessimistic to do so. However, a number do include it, explaining that:

- the constantly changing business environment means that redundancy is occasionally inevitable, but the organisation will do its utmost to find other solutions first
- wherever possible, employees will be redeployed

● where this is impossible, support will be made available in the following forms...

References

Some companies include information about what references they require or may pass on.

Disciplinary and grievance procedures

(Some organisations might include harassment in this section rather than relate it to equal opportunities.)

You may want to make it clear that disciplinary and grievance procedures are not contractual, in terms of something along the lines of 'This section is for information only and does not form part of your contract of employment.' See Chapter 5, Legal Aspects.

Discipline

Introduce and outline the disciplinary procedure. Explain that the emphasis is on correcting unsatisfactory conduct before it becomes too serious.

This is a procedure that is particularly suited to being set out in a flowchart. You may want to say who is authorised to dismiss staff.

Some employers list examples of behaviour that will be construed as 'acts of gross misconduct' and result in instant dismissal. Make sure it is clear that this list is not exclusive.

Poor performance

Outline your organisation's procedures for dealing with poor performance.

Appeals and grievances

This is another procedure that lends itself well to being described in a flowchart.

Remuneration and benefits

Salary management

Include information on the job evaluation system – if it is based on competencies, include a summary list of them here – and the grading structure.

Salary reviews

State how often salaries are reviewed (usually annually) and when the review is effective from. If there is an award that is applied to all staff (eg negotiated with a union or a cost-of-living adjustment), say so. If consistently excellent per-formers receive more than the standard increase, say so too. Some organisations also like to state that other adjust-ments may also be made (usually in order to ensure that personnel policies are operating properly – policies such as equal pay for equal-value work, consistency of salaries, the job has grown and/or includes more responsibility, market rates have changed). Some organisations specifically state that they reserve the right to reduce pay (eg as a result of poor performance) or 'red circle' pay (eg where an individ-ual has somehow become 'overpaid' with respect to col-leagues).

Payment of salaries

State what information the payslip contains, and what deductions may have been made. Describe when (eg the last

Thursday of every month) and how (eg 'directly into your bank account, Giro account or building society') salaries are paid. If you nominate a date (eg the 20th of each month) rather than a weekday, you must remember to explain what happens if the banks are shut on that date. Some organisations disclaim responsibility for the length of time taken by the financial service appointed by employees as the destination for salary transfers to credit their accounts.

Profit-share, bonus schemes, share option schemes

These schemes vary enormously from organisation to organisation. The rules may be set out in another document, but it is useful to tell employees how they can qualify for each scheme, and when payments are likely to be made. You may also wish explicitly to state that the directors of the organisation reserve the right to alter or cancel the scheme.

Pensions

You may feel that this subject links more logically together with retirement: that is up to you. Wherever you put it, you should state whether or not your organisation offers a pension scheme and who is entitled to join. Further details will be contained within a separate document: you should explain how employees can get a copy, and who they should speak to if they need further information or if they need to give information concerning a change in dependants.

Overtime

Details may be included in the letter of appointment. Explain how a claim for overtime should be submitted (by a certain time, on a particular form, to a particular person or department).

Tax

This is the place to say that your organisation does not accept any responsibility for the tax liability of staff, and to outline the procedures for making PAYE (pay as you earn) deductions.

National Insurance

Outline the contributions for which employees are liable, and add any other helpful information.

Expenses

State that staff are entitled to be reimbursed for all necessary expenditure incurred in the course of their employment. Outline the procedures for claiming expenses. Some organisations provide company credit cards to be used exclusively for business expenses – the rules covering the use of these cards must be spelled out.

Some employers specifically state that knowingly submitting a false claim for expenses is to be regarded as gross misconduct, for which the penalty is summary dismissal – and also that failure to account for an advance against expenses within a reasonable period is a disciplinary offence.

Loans and advances

Describe how the organisation is willing to help in the following situations:

- an employee needs a reference for a loan or mortgage, opening a bank account, submitting a rental application, etc
- an employee needs a loan to help pay for season tickets

- a rare case of unforeseeable financial hardship.

One-off payments, eg long service, marriage, etc

Quite a lot of organisations give either a tax-free gift or paid holidays, or cash, or a mixture of all these after 25 years' service or when an employee gets married. 'Young' companies, and those employing predominantly younger people, make long-service awards after much shorter times – sometimes as little as five years.

Maternity

Most organisations' provisions are based on statutory requirements and are described in a separate document which includes information also about leave.

Company cars

The full regulations regarding drivers' obligations and responsibilities are usually better covered in a separate document. However, it may be helpful to state here who administers the scheme, and to remind employees that a company car represents a benefit-in-kind and is subject to income tax.

Childcare support

Describe any of the following that your organisation provides:

- workplace nurseries
- holiday-time play schemes
- emergency crèche facilities
- in-house childcare information and advice
- working parents advice.

Travelling on business

The use of privately owned cars

State the allowances that may be made if an individual is authorised to use his or her own car on your organisation's business. If it is a regular arrangement, the individual should inform his or her insurance company whether your organisation's cover is third-party only.

Travel and subsistence allowances

Some organisations guarantee specific allowances – *subsistence allowances* – for personal expenses incurred while an employee is away on business. These allowances may include such items as a newspaper, cinema ticket, alcoholic drink with dinner, etc. Sometimes they include hotel costs; sometimes these are paid directly by the employer. Sometimes an allowance is paid if the employee stays with friends. In any case, these allowances are subject to tax unless previously agreed with your organisation's tax inspector. State your organisation's stance, and describe how the allowance should be claimed.

Relocation

When an employee is required to move house, either within the UK or internationally, your organisation may have a relocation policy set out in a separate document (international moves in particular can be incredibly complex) or in its absence may wish to negotiate any financial assistance offered on an individual basis.

Career development

State your company's commitment to the development of staff. Also state (if indeed it is the case) that staff are responsible for their own development – the initiative for development should generally come from the individual, and the means of further development (secondments, projects) other than training courses should be considered first.

Performance appraisal

Explain the purpose of your organisation's appraisal system. Best practice is to align personal, departmental and corporate objectives, and to facilitate a mechanism for learning from the past in order to improve the future.

Details of the appraisal scheme are quite often available separately (they are often summarised on the front cover of the appraisal form, or included in an employee's appraisal documentation binder). However, you may wish to say in the handbook when and how often appraisals take place, and how to obtain more information on their use.

Training

Describe the internal training resources that are available, and also the organisation's policy in relation to external training and further education (in particular to day-release courses).

The hiring process

Many organisations outline the procedures they use for recruitment. See *Appendix 2: Scope* at the back of the book and the procedures used there.

Promotion

Describe the system for internal promotion and the advertisement of internal vacancies.

Secondments and attachments

If the organisation is big enough, arrangements can sometimes be made to enable staff to gain work experience that they would not get in their current job. (For more information, see the IPD's Information Note on secondments.)

If the organisation is a member of a body such as Business in the Community (see *Useful Organisations* at the back of this book) which arranges secondments to charities, this is the place to explain what opportunities of this kind there are for employees. If employees are expected to carry out this kind of work in their own time, it should be clearly stated.

Intellectual property

Patents, inventions and designs

State your organisation's policy regarding the ownership of ideas and inventions developed by an individual and/or team working during the organisation's paid time.

Information technology

E-mail policy

Your e-mail policy should have a named contact for both training and e-mail management. See Appendix 1 at the back of this book for an example of how British Airways has tackled this subject.

Internet use

Make clear who is allowed access, what information can be downloaded, and what the provisions are against undue web 'browsing'.

Equal opportunities

The statement you make should cover both current employees and job applicants. An equal opportunities policy should determine that no one will receive less favourable treatment on the grounds of sex, marital status, religious creed, colour, race or ethnic origin. You may want to make it clear that these procedures are not contractual, saying something along the lines of 'This section is for information only and does not form part of your contract of employment.' See Chapter 5, Legal aspects.

Harassment

It is against the law to harass another person. You may wish to state that your organisation is opposed to it in any form. Outline the procedures here or in a separate document. Consult the IPD *Good Practice Guide* on *Bullying and Sexual Harassment* for further information (see the bibliography).

Bullying

It is estimated that 1 in 30 people is a bully, and bullying has now become a recognised and significant problem in the workplace. Because there is, so far, no law against bullying, it's particularly important to include a written statement about it in your policies and procedures, and include it in your list of gross misconduct offences. See 'Success

Unlimited's web site (see the bibliography).

Personal liability

Insurance

If your organisation offers insurance against any of the following, it should be covered under a section on *Benefits*:

- long-term disability
- health problems
- unexpected death
- a necessity for emergency dental treatment
- personal accident
- travel difficulties and losses.

Personal property

You may wish to state that employees are responsible for their own personal property and that the organisation does not accept any liability or responsibility for damage to or loss of individual employees' property.

Health and safety at work

A written health and safety policy is a legal requirement for organisations with five or more employees and should comply with the Health and Safety at Work Act (HASAW) 1974.

General statement

Health and safety is the responsibility of everyone in an organisation.

Safety

Quote all relevant safety regulations.

In the event of a fire

You may wish to outline procedures to undertake in the event of a fire.

Hygiene

Quote the hygiene regulations relevant to your organisation.

Health checks

Outline the arrangements your organisation has for checking up on the health of its employees.

Alcohol

In many workplaces the consumption of alcohol is allowed only at specific authorised events (celebrations, leaving parties, etc). Most employers reckon that to find an employee to be under the influence of alcohol when at work is, at the least, a serious disciplinary matter. This is particularly the case if the employee is required to operate machinery or drive a car, or is in any way liable to pose a threat to general health and safety as a result of his or her drinking. The *Good Practice Guide* on *Drugs and Alcohol Policies* (see bibliography at the back of this book) covers this, and the subject below, in full.

Drugs

Normally, employees found in possession of or under the influence of non-prescribed drugs are subject, at the least, to disciplinary action. Many employers include the posses-sion of, or an offer to supply or produce, controlled drugs in the list of offences for which an employee can be summar-ily dismissed. You should outline exactly what measures your organisation would take in this situation.

AIDS (Acquired immune-deficiency syndrome)

You may wish to state that your organisation does not dis-criminate or allow discrimination against staff on the grounds either of their being HIV-positive or of having fully-developed AIDS.

Smoking policy

If your organisation has a smoking policy, you should state clearly:

- whether it is a contractual matter (if it is, that should be included in the offer letter)
- (if it is not a contractual matter) the areas in which smoking is permitted.

The *Good Practice Guide* on *Smoking Policies* (see the bibliogra-phy at the back of this book) covers this in full.

Wellness programme

Outline your organisation's wellness programme, if any.

Accidents and first-aid treatment

Accidents, injuries and 'dangerous occurrences' at work must, by law, be officially recorded. Clearly state where the Accident Book – the government-required document for the purpose – is to be found. Details of trained first-aiders should be easily available – on notice-boards and through department heads (and their secretaries) and the personnel function.

Counselling service

Outline your organisation's counselling service, if any.

Employee communications

This is the place to make a general statement that the organisation is aiming at multidirectional communication, and that employees are encouraged to make their opinions and suggestions known – in a constructive way.

Some organisations clearly tell their employees that they have a responsibility to keep themselves informed and up to date about corporate developments.

Corporate publications

Give details of the publications that your organisation produces, including publications for customers as well as for staff. Some organisations also distribute their annual report and accounts.

Meetings

Outline the overall company approach to staff meetings, or describe the team briefing system, if any.

Intranet

Outline the information that is available on the intranet, if your organisation has one.

Notice-boards

You may wish to describe the use of notice-boards as a means of keeping staff informed.

Personal records

For every single employee the organisation needs an up-to-date contact name and contact details for emergencies. Employees should also give information about changes of address, etc.

Data protection

Under the Data Protection Act 1998, staff have certain rights to see information which relates to them. If your organisation has specific procedures for obtaining such information, set them out here.

Employment of relatives or people with whom there are close personal ties

If your organisation has a policy on this, describe it here. Some organisations specifically decree that no one should have any authority over anyone who is a relative or with whom they have close personal ties.

Employee voice

Trade unions

Where trade unions are recognised, their role should be described clearly in the handbook.

Suggestion schemes

Describe your organisation's suggestion scheme(s), including details of any rewards given.

Social

Clubs

List the sports and social clubs available to employees, and give membership details.

Facilities

Describe the medical, canteen, parking and transport facilities your organisation offers.

Support of charities

If your organisation supports a specific charity or charities, explain the rationale behind the choice, and describe the support given.

Dress code or uniforms

A can of worms! It's often easier to fudge the issue by saying something along the lines of 'Staff should dress appropriately.' Easier still to leave it out altogether. If your organisation has 'plain-clothes' or 'casual' days, then this is the right place to include information about it.

5

Legal aspects

☑ What does the law require?
☑ What are the legal advantages of staff handbooks?
☑ What are the legal pitfalls?

The policies and procedures outlined within a staff hand-book must comply with the laws of the country within which the organisation is operating. This is not as straight-forward as it sounds. Laws covering health and safety, employment, tax and many other matters are complex. It is advisable to have a legal expert look over the text of a staff handbook before the document is distributed.

What does the law require?

The employee handbook is also a legal document in its own right. An organisation is required (by the Employment Rights Act [ERA] 1996) to give all employees a statement of the terms and conditions of their employment within two months of their joining the organisation. The legislation allows this written statement to refer employees on to other documents to which they have reasonable access in respect of certain items, specifically:

- sickness provisions
- pensions
- notice periods
- specific disciplinary and/or grievance matters.

If the handbook is to be referred to in the written statement, it is advisable to get employees to sign a form to indicate that they have received their own personal copy.

What are the legal advantages of staff handbooks?

One of the advantages of staff handbooks is that they make
it possible to keep contracts of employment to a reasonable
length. They are also helpful change management tools in
that they are easier to update than the main statement of
terms and conditions required by law.

Remember, too, that your organisation already has policies and procedures, in the form of its personnel practices,
even if there is nothing formal in writing. These personnel
practices represent precedents that could be upheld in a
court of law. There is further advantage in ensuring that your
personnel practices are documented in the way you may
want a court to interpret them rather than in a way in which
someone might try to score a point over the organisation.

What are the legal pitfalls?

Inevitably, there are dangers. It has always been important
to draw a clear distinction between the contractual rights
of an employee and his or her non-contractual rights. This
can be easily done by placing them in separate sections.

66

Through case-law, however, this has recently become even more important.

Staff handbooks generally contain two types of information: contractually binding information – such as holiday arrangements and sick pay entitlements – and general information, such as the emergency fire procedure, the company policy on cars, or what the social club does. Difficulties arise when it is not clear what is and what is not contractual. The policies and procedures to be particularly wary of are:

- disciplinary
- grievance handling
- equal opportunities.

The following example illustrates why the distinction is important.

Company A has not made it clear that its disciplinary procedure is not contractual. The procedure specifies that an employee should have three days' advance notice of a disciplinary interview. The managers involved fail to follow the procedure exactly. Only two days' notice is given – but the employee is dismissed nonetheless.

The employee argues that the disciplinary procedure is contractual, and that it forms part of his terms and conditions. The employer denies this, and says that it is there purely for information and guidance.

The final judgement, however, is made by the tribunal. If the tribunal decides in favour of the employer, it may express concern that the procedure wasn't followed but will declare that there has been no breach of contract. However, if the tribunal decides in favour of the employee, then, technically, the employer must be in breach of contract.

In previous times this was not a matter for too much concern, for the court would simply estimate the extra time the procedure should have taken (only one day in this case) and compensate the employee with the earnings due for that time.

Now, however, courts are beginning to make the calculation on an entirely different basis (see *Raspin* v *United News Shops Ltd* [1999] IRLR 9). Their new approach is to reason that if the disciplinary procedure had been correctly followed, the employee might have kept his job. The compensation is then based on an estimate of the length of time the employee would be likely to take in getting a new job (say one year) and an estimate of how likely the decision to dismiss is of being upheld (say 50 per cent). The employee would then get *half a year's* salary as compensation!

One way to ensure that this does not happen is to add some such clause as 'This policy/procedure is for information only: it does not form part of your terms and conditions of employment.'

One of the purposes of a handbook is to make staff aware of how they ought to be treated under various procedures, and thus help to reduce the possibility of employment tribunal claims. By getting it checked over for the legal niceties you can ensure that your handbook is indeed an asset – rather than a liability, as it might have been.

6

Marketing your staff handbook

> ☑ Market research
>   Identify your market – Establish your budget and
>   deadlines – Primary versus secondary research –
>   Secondary research – Benchmark – Primary research
> ☑ Internal marketing
>   Write a marketing plan – Situation analysis –
>   Create a balanced mix of compelling promotions –
>   Train and brief – Measure the response
> ☑ Distribution

There was a time when employee communications con-
sisted of reluctantly deciding that the staff should maybe be
told that the plant was closing/was moving/had been
bought. No longer. Employee communications have
changed from being purely a matter of passing information
down, and then from including some employee involvement, to emerge as full-scale internal marketing. Internal
marketing means considering your staff to be a market like
any other market. The perception you are most likely to
have to turn on its head is the one that the handbook rep-

resents nothing more than a whole lot of uninteresting rules and regulations imposed from above. Instead, you want people to understand that they can benefit greatly from using your handbook: it is a source of valuable information and guidance.

If you have any marketing professionals (not salespeople) in your organisation, try to enlist their help. Make it clear to them that you are not asking so much for their help with the hard graft as looking more for their professional advice, and most especially for their *ideas* – an area which most marketing people really enjoy and excel at. Try to arrange an informal session with them, preferably away from the office, where you have a better chance of getting their full attention. Before you go, brief yourself on some basic marketing concepts (read Robert Grede's paperback *Naked Marketing* – see the bibliography at the back of this book).

The purpose of marketing is to satisfy needs and wants. This may seem obvious. People are rarely interested in things they don't need and don't want. Unfortunately, it's not always obvious what they do need and do want.

There's only one way to find out – and that is by doing some market research.

Market research

If 'market research' sounds like a lengthy, expensive and even boring process, think again. It doesn't have to be. The market research can be the most fascinating part of the whole process – and what's more, you can use the results just as beneficially to help with many other projects. It doesn't have to cost a lot or take up much time, especially if it's well planned.

Identify your market

Be clear, right from the start, about exactly who your market is. Is this handbook intended for the personnel department, for managers, for employees, or for everybody? Who 'owns' the staff handbook? Is it the chief executive, the board, or the personnel department? What is the purpose of the handbook for the users, and for the sponsors? It is at this stage that you need to carry out a little initial lobbying, especially with senior managers. Some tips for getting influencers on side are shown below.

Getting senior management support

1 Calculate the costs
One of the first things senior managers are going to ask is 'How much is it going to cost?' As long as it does not come to an unreasonable amount (the main cost is in terms of time), the point here is that you have given it thought and made provision for it in an appropriate budget.

Clear procedures and policies for controlling absence, poor performance, etc, can also clearly be seen to result in cost savings, but these are very difficult to quantify. Some senior managers may ask for a Return on Investment (ROI) calculation – they are expecting the new policies and handbook to pay for themselves within two years. Frankly, I am dubious about the value of spending time in making such calculations: the input is so subjective.

2 Use 'hooks' – say what's in it for them
Look over the benefits of having a staff handbook as outlined in Chapter 1. Choose those most likely to appeal to your senior management. State clearly, using all media, and repeat frequently! Remember to sell the benefits (what it will do for

---

them), *not* the features (a straightforward description).

3 *Show need*
Identify why the senior managers *need* the handbook. Give examples, situations, or problems which may be resolved by having a handbook.

4 *Ensure that you really consult*
Consulting does not mean simply explaining what you plan to do and asking for approval. Real consulting means presenting alternatives – 'Do you want the ethics policy to be detailed specifically, or left open to interpretation?'

5 *Lobby!*
Bend the ear of those who influence senior managers. If there is a senior-level champion appointed for this project, enlist his or her enthusiastic help.

6 *Choose your moment*
Obvious, this one! Don't go crashing into a board meeting about cost-cutting and put your handbook proposal to them. Check meeting agendas first.

7 *Are you a prophet in your own country?*
Sometimes in-house professionals don't hold quite the same amount of sway as external consultants. This is more often than not based on pure prejudice and is entirely unfair, but it does happen. If this is the case, enlist the help of an external consultant.

Establish your budget and deadlines

What resources do you have for marketing, in terms of both finance and staff? What are the deadlines for the different stages of the process? Make sure these are incorporated into the overall project plan (see Chapter 2).

Primary *versus* secondary research

There are two types of research: *primary* and *secondary*. Think back to your school days. Remember having to write a project on Tropical Rain Forests? You couldn't fly out to the Amazon delta, so all your research had to be *secondary* research. If you had been able to go out and experiment and observe at first hand, that would have been *primary* research.

Secondary research

It's usually best to start with the secondary research. Secondary research results in your being better informed when you come to the 'live' interviews or group sessions involved with primary research. It also means that you are able to put together a more focused and useful set of questions to ask. Within your organisation (most likely within your computer systems) you have a wealth of information. From your personnel records you may be able to print out age and sex profiles. You can reap rich harvests of information from staff attitude surveys, feedback forms from team-briefing meetings, training manuals (eg comments on the format of the manual or handout).

Benchmark

In addition to internal research, also conduct external research. Collect as many examples of other organisations' handbooks as you can. If you're an IPD member, spend a day at the IPD library, where there is quite an extensive collection, and make notes or copies of anything you think would work particularly well for your organisation. Surf the Internet. Quite a lot of organisations publish their handbooks on their websites.

Primary research

Research for a staff handbook must also include primary research. You get valuable information from primary research, but you also increase your chances of enthusiastic buy-in. People are more likely to identify with a project if they have been consulted. So before writing a word of your handbook carry out primary research of your market – find out what *they* need, what *they* would find useful, and find out why.

You can do this in a number of different ways, for example:

- structured individual interviews, either by phone or face to face
- focus groups
- a paper survey
- an e-mail survey
- analysis of information held on current staff – age profiles, geographic spread, access to equipment, education, likes and dislikes (engineers, for example, often tend to like diagrams and flowcharts).

Never undertake an unstructured interview. You will waste everyone's time including your own, and lose a lot of credibility in the process. You may forget to ask something vital, and you won't be able to make comparisons objectively or identify majority opinions or requirements (eg 'Nine out of ten confirmed that they liked the proposed title' or 'Only one of the 15 wanted a loose-leaf format'). Think the questions through. It's sometimes helpful to have a list of prompts. Try the questionnaire out on a supportive colleague. Time your interview, and aim for an average of 15-

20 minutes per interview – any longer and people might start to get restive and think of other things they need to do. Make sure you write up (or better still, type or print out) your notes as soon after the interview as possible. Hastily scribbled notes soon become totally indecipherable.

Sample questions for a structured interview

1 Which of the following titles do you like best? (Those below are just examples. If you have a list of five or six, you might want to ask your interviewees to prioritise them.)

- *Xyz Company Staff Handbook*
- *Information for Staff*
- *Xyzcode* or *The Xyz Way* (a handbook 'brandname').

2 What would you use the handbook for?

3 When and where would you use the handbook?

4 What do you think is good about our current handbook? (or: What works well for you about our current handbook?)

5 What is not good?/What doesn't work?

6 Would you prefer:

- ring-binder?
- a bound publication?
- a computer disk?

(Make sure you suggest only what you are willing to offer: ring-binders may be too expensive, and computer disks may not satisfy the legal criteria.)

Ensure that you find out:

- what information they would like included, what subject areas they would like covered

- the format they would like for the handbook – for example, on the intranet, in a ring-binder, etc
- how often they think it should be revised
- what back-up they would like to be available to support the handbook (for example, who they should contact to clarify a point or give details about a policy)
- how would they like it distributed (whether they each need their own copy, or whether it is sufficient to have a reference copy easily accessible for each department)
- what benefits and advantages they look for in having a staff handbook – and get them to prioritise these.

Consult the following:

- anyone with responsibility for specific matters covered in the handbook (eg the PR manager in respect of the section on dealing with the media, the accounts manager in respect of the payment of salaries, etc)
- trade union or other employee representatives
- the lawyer(s) who will be checking the completed draft
- senior management.

Internal marketing

Write a marketing plan

Good organisation is just as essential for this part of the project as for any other. Whether you are in a large or a small organisation, put yourself to the discipline of writing down what you hope to achieve, what you intend to do, and how it is to be done.

Situation analysis

Begin with a situation analysis. Write a description of your market, an assessment of the media available, and a note about how other similar campaigns have succeeded or failed (what works well and what doesn't in your organisation).

Create a balanced mix of compelling promotions

Use media designed to penetrate all possible target markets for the least cost. Your research has given you a wealth of information about your market (or markets): the trick is now to match the market to the media. The following media are among those traditionally used for promoting a new staff handbook:

- in-house publications
- team-briefing sessions
- roadshows
- intranet website
- notice-boards.

Then think creatively. How are you going to grab the attention of the market? Read the account at the back of this book of the introduction of a new e-mail policy (*E-mail delivers better results in British Airways*). It used a mix of all kinds of media – an impressively large-scale campaign – but small companies can be just as creative and effective.

Train and brief

Train and brief those who are going to front up your campaign. Make sure they have all the materials they need and that presentation is as easy and smooth for them to undertake as possible.

Measure the response

One of the major advantages to producing your handbook on the organisation's intranet is that you can ask for feedback on the new handbook, and it's easy for people to e-mail their response to you using a standard questionnaire format. It is also easy and cheap then to incorporate their comments and suggestions straight away, rather than have to wait two or three years for a reprint.

Distribution

Everybody in the organisation should either receive their own personal copy of your handbook or have easy access to it. If some contractual items are included in the text, it's advisable to get each employee either to sign for his or her handbook or to confirm in writing that he or she has seen and got access to the handbook (see what Scope does, in *Appendix 2* at the back of this book). In large organisations, the logistics of the distribution require careful thought. One approach that is known to work successfully is to distribute the handbook at a series of briefing or training sessions. This way, people understand its uses and benefits better, and are more likely to get into the habit of using it right from the beginning.

What's most important is that no one is left out – something that could have a very isolating and demotivating effect on some individuals.

Bibliography

Legal

Copies of legislation such as the Health and Safety at Work Act 1974, the Data Protection Act 1998, the Employment Rights Act 1996, can be obtained either from the Stationery Office, or from the website www.hmso.gov.uk.

There is also an enormous amount of free information and links about employment legislation on DiscLaw Publishing Limited's website, www.emplaw.co.uk. DiscLaw's hard-copy publications are also available through the Law Society.

Written Statement of Employment Particulars. Booklet PL700, Department of Trade and Industry.

If the handbook is to be used as one of the documents referred to in the employees' written statement of terms and conditions, this is a useful document to consult.

Content

Scope has produced two documents: the *Personnel Procedures Quality Manual* and *The Induction Manual: Your guide to working with Scope,* available for £125 and £50 respectively.

Information Notes. London, Institute of Personnel and Development.

This series is available from the IPD either in printed form or on the IPD's website, www.ipd.co.uk. Current titles include:

No 1 *Developing an E-mail Policy*
No 8 *Business Gifts*
No 9 *Induction*
No 18 *Bullying at Work*
No 19 *Internet Policies*
No 20 *References*
No 21 *Profit-related Pay.*

Good Practice series. London, Institute of Personnel and Development.

Aside from *Creating a Staff Handbook*, the others in this series are:

Bullying and Sexual Harassment
Drugs and Alcohol Policies
Induction
Part-time Workers
Smoking Policies.

Best Practice series. London, The Industrial Society.

These include sample documents, case-studies, etc. Back issues include:

No 12 *Mentoring*
No 26 *Managing Ethics*
No 34 *Flexible Benefits*
No 44 *Benchmarking Human Resources*
No 57 *Managing Discipline and Grievance.*

Changing Times - A guide to flexible work patterns for human resource managers. London, New Ways to Work, 1993.

This is a practical manual to help managers to implement a range of flexible working options including part-time, job-sharing, flexitime, term-time working, career breaks, annual hours and working from home.

ISHMAEL A. *and* ALEMORU B. *Harassment, Bullying and Violence at Work – A practical guide to combating employee abuse*. London, The Industrial Society, 1999.
A practical book with lots of case studies and advice on policy and strategy development.

About writing handbooks

ACAS. *The Company Handbook*. London, ACAS, 1997.

Copy-writing

CAREY G. V. *Mind the Stop*. Harmondsworth, Penguin Books, 1971.
CUTTS M. *The Plain English Guide*. Oxford, Oxford University Press, 1996.
The Economist Style Guide. Bath, Bath University Press, 1998.
HOPKINS B. *How to Design and Post Information on a Corporate Intranet*. London, Gower, 1997.

Intranets

KILIAN C. *Writing for the Web*. Self Counsel Press Inc, 1999.
WILLIAMS R. *and* TOLLETT J. *The Non-Designers Web Book*. Peachpit Press, 1998.

Managing groups

HARDINGHAM A. *Working in Teams*. London, Institute of Personnel and Development, 1998.

MARSH J. *and* SUMSION M. *Chairing Meetings*. South East Employers, 1998.

PARSLOE E. *The Manager as Coach and Mentor*. 2nd edn. London, Institute of Personnel and Development, 1999.

Managing projects

BEE R. *and* F. *Project Management: The people challenge*. London, Institute of Personnel and Development, 1997.

Internal marketing

FORMAN S. *and* MONEY A. *Internal Marketing*. Henley, Henley Management College, 1995.

GREDE R. *Naked Marketing*. Hemel Hempstead, Prentice Hall, 1999.

This pocket-guide to marketing provides practical basics for people who need to quickly understand and apply marketing techniques. It offers sound examples useful in almost any business.

THOMSON K. *and* WHITWELL K. *Managing Your Internal Customers*. London, Financial Times/Pitman Publishing, 1993.

Making presentations

BOWMAN L. *High-Impact Business Presentations*. London, Century Business, 1991.

SIDDONS S. *Presentation Skills*. 2nd edn. London, Institute of Personnel and Development, 1999.

Useful organisations

**Institute of Personnel and Development
Consultancy Service**
IPD House
Camp Road
London
SW19 4UX
Tel: 020–8971 9000
Fax: 020–8263 3344
e-mail: consult@ipd.co.uk
Website: www.ipd.co.uk

Can recommend consultants to help with the formulation
and writing of employee handbooks.

Ruth Allan
New Ways to Work
309 Upper Street
London
N1 2TY
Tel: 020–7226 4026
Fax: 020–7354 2978

New Ways to Work is an independent organisation which
promotes a wide range of flexible work patterns, produces
publications and offers training and consultancy services
on flexible working.

The Industrial Society and The Employee Communications Association

49 Calthorpe Road
Quadrant Court
Edgbaston
Birmingham
B15 1TH
Tel: 0121–410 3000
Fax: 0121–410 3333
Website: www.indsoc.co.uk

The Industrial Society provides a *Best Practice Direct* service that presents a practical easy-to-use guide to benchmarking, with examples of best-practice documentation and short case notes on how each document is used. The Employee Communications Association provides a forum for employers on employee communications strategies and techniques.

The Institute of Business Ethics

12 Palace Street
London
SW1E 5JA
Tel: 020–7931 0495
Fax: 020–7821 5819
Website: www.ibe.org.uk

Provides employers with advice and information on ethics policies.

Tim Field
Success Unlimited
PO Box 67
Didcot
Oxfordshire
OX11 0YH
Tel: 01235–834548
Fax: 01235–861721
Website: www.successunlimited.co.uk

A marvellous website which covers all kinds of information on bullying and harassment.

Business in the Community
44 Baker Street
London
W1M 1DH
Tel: 020–7224 1600
Fax: 020–7486 1700
Website: www.bitc.org.uk

Offers information, contacts, etc, and runs workshops on secondments within the community.

Software suppliers

Flowcharts

Visio
Vision International (UK) Ltd
64/74 East Street
Epsom
Surrey
KT17 1HE
Tel: 01372–847800
Fax: 01372–847900
Website: www.visio.com

Desktop publishing

QuarkExpress (probably the most likely to be compatible
with your printer's equipment):

Quark Systems Ltd
20 Quarry Street
Guildford
Surrey
GU1 3UY
Tel: 01483–445566
Fax: 01483–445544
Website: www.quark.com

Adobe PageMaker
Freepost EH3314
PO Box 12350
Edinburgh
EH11 0NR
Tel: 0131–458 6842
Fax: 0131–451 6999
Website: www.adobe.com

Microsoft Publisher
Microsoft Ltd
Microsoft Place
Winnersh
Wokingham
Berkshire
RG41 5TP
Tel: 0870–601 0100
Fax: 0870–602 0100
Website: www.microsoft.com

Web-authoring

Adobe PageMill
Freepost EH3314
PO Box 12350
Edinburgh
EH11 0NR
Tel: 0131–458 6842
Fax: 0131–451 6999
Website: www.adobe.com

FileMaker
FileMaker Inc
5201 Patrick Henry Drive
Santa Clara
CA 95052–8168
USA
Tel: [001] 408–987 7000
Website: www.filemaker.com

Appendix 1: British Airways

A brave new business world

The year 1999 rings in a host of new commercial challenges as we strive to reconcile some fundamental contradictions. Global networks create instant communication, yet they overload people with too much information to understand. Databases enable one-to-one marketing with customers while relationships with people inside organisations are breaking down. Change is driving inefficiency out of business but also driving out people's commitment.

Reconciling these contradictions demands more than conventional approaches. This special report offers new ways of thinking about classic problems like information overload and emerging challenges like Y2K and EMU. We hope you'll use the enclosed reply card to let us know the challenges you'd like addressed in future issues!

E-mail delivers better results in British Airways

More than 2 million e-mails a week threatened to overload British Airways' networks and its people. BA asked MCA Live to help staff solve the problem.

'Most e-mail systems are like Formula One racing-cars that never get out of first gear because people haven't really learned how to use them,' says MCA senior consultant Catherine Foster. Caroline Gatenby, service manager at British Airways agrees: 'We wanted to keep up the enthusiasm for using e-mail, but channel it into best practices.'

BA was moving from three different e-mail systems to a single system, and saw a chance to encourage more effective e-mail habits. Convincing staff to learn a new e-mail system and better e-mail practices required a strong call to action.

Caroline explains. 'We needed to get people's attention and appeal to everyone using e-mail, which is a very wide and sophisticated audience. We had to change attitudes and behaviours to address the underlying causes of our e-mail overload and get the long-term benefit of our system.'

According to Marc Wright, managing director of MCA Live and lead partner on the project, the key was to develop messages people could connect with by keeping things light and clear. The vital messages were launched in an internal campaign:

- *The Daily E-mail*, a paper-based newspaper with headlines like 'Thousands Feared Buried in E-Quake' was widely circulated. 'People just loved it,' remembers Caroline. Marc adds: 'Clever headlines got people to pick it up. Then we used humour to keep them reading about valuable e-mail tips.'

Navigating the information superhighway

Remember the good old days when we thought the Internet and e-mail would give us more time? Today, the average employee handles at least 169 e-mails each day, according to a study by Pitney Bowes. Some new voice-recognition systems even send and receive e-mails through your mobile phone!

The bottom line is that the information superhighway has us in the middle of a traffic jam of data. With Y2K problems looming, we may be skidding into the world's biggest crash.

The solution? We believe it lies in focusing on the principles of effective communication instead of the systems of communications. This means providing strategic direction, setting clear standards and ensuring that people have the skills they need. We wouldn't put a new driver on the road with any less!

- A short video satirised some common e-mail habits that can overly burden the system – such as leaving an in-box overflowing with e-mails, or sending extremely large files as attachments.
- A touring exhibition around Heathrow and Gatwick included the video, rolling presentations,

and a PC clinic with five-minute 'ability boosters'. 'All we needed was more advance marketing to promote the exhibition,' says Caroline. 'Otherwise, it worked really well for people to experience things for themselves.'

- A questionnaire given to people at the exhibition explored their use of e-mail. A few months later, several hundred of those originally surveyed volunteered to complete another form. Their responses show a clear change in behaviour as a result of the campaign. The number of people who send fewer than 30 e-mails each day has increased 17 per cent, and the number of people who receive more than 30 e-mails each day has decreased by 7 per cent. The survey also shows that e-mails are becoming more relevant and better written.
- System changes made it easier for people to follow best practice. For example, departmental logos at the top of e-mails took up a lot of memory, so they were replaced with separate and much simpler headers.

Caroline says that BA is clearly learning the art of e-mail. 'The feedback has been very positive. People are even talking with their colleagues now about unnecessarily long e-mails and non-business use.'

Old habits die hard, so BA continues to present smaller versions of the exhibition around the world and reminds people of good e-mail habits through its intranet site. BA's approach proves that an ounce of prevention is worth a pound of cure.

For more information, please contact Catherine Foster at MCA's Marlow office on [+44] (0)1628–473217.

Appendix 2: Scope

Document control

Each copy of the *Personnel Procedures Quality Manual* is uniquely identified, and the holder's name is registered with the Management Services Division, which is responsible for document control.

It is the responsibility of the registered manual holder to ensure that the contents remain correct and up to date. The manual is reviewed on a regular basis: revisions and updates will be issued to registered holders, along with a Document Control Revision List. Records of all amendments are maintained by Human Resources Division, at Market Road, London.

Holders of the manual are requested to return their manual when leaving or changing their position in Scope.

Only controlled copies will be maintained. Any copies of the controlled document should be marked 'copy': these will not be maintained through the controlled manual system and may therefore not be the current issue.

Comments or queries relating to the content of this manual should be referred to any personnel officer within Scope. Your feedback is welcome, and if you have any spe-

cific suggestions for improvements to the policies, procedures or layout of this manual, please use the feedback
form provided, addressed to Scope's Executive Director of
Human Resources.

Induction: action plan

With your line manager and your colleagues, this action
plan should be used to structure your first few weeks. It is
an important opportunity for you to meet colleagues in
other parts of the organisation and to look at different
aspects of your work. At the end of the induction period you
will be asked to reflect on what you have learned and to
report back to your line manager.

The action plan comprises the following record sheets for
you to complete as your induction progresses:

- timetable
- objectives
- learning log
- contacts outside your division.

This section also contains information about your proba-
tion period and performance appraisal.

Aims of induction

At the end of your induction you should be able to talk about:

- how what you do helps towards achieving Scope's
  Mission
- what your team and department aim to achieve
  this year

- cerebral palsy, and how it affects the lives of individuals
- national and local projects, and the range of services and activities for people with cerebral palsy that we are involved in
- your role: the people you will be working with, what they do, and who your main contacts are in other parts of the organisation.

Introduction

The purpose of Scope's recruitment and selection procedure is to ensure that there is consistency when recruiting staff to join Scope, that any form of illegal discrimination is avoided, and that accepted good practice is followed.

The prime consideration of a recruitment and selection panel is to ensure that the best candidate is chosen for the job regardless of disability, race, gender, religion, or sexual orientation, in line with Scope's equal opportunities policy.

In order to achieve this aim, it is important that everyone concerned with the recruitment and selection process has a clear understanding of the job to be filled, its requirement, and the attributes of the likely job-holder in terms of skills, qualifications, previous experience, etc.

Managerial guidance and *appropriate* training will be provided to support this procedure.

Recruitment to posts within Scope

```
┌─────────────────────────────────────┐          ┌─────────────────────────────────┐
│  Established post becomes vacant     │          │  New post is created and approved│
└─────────────────────────────────────┘          │           by EMB                │
                    ▼                             └─────────────────────────────────┘
┌─────────────────────────────────────┐
│ Job description and person specification
│ are written and evaluated if a new post,  ◄──────────────────────┘
│  or reviewed if an established post  │
└─────────────────────────────────────┘
                    ▼
┌─────────────────────────────────────┐
│      Advertisement is written        │
└─────────────────────────────────────┘
                    ▼
┌─────────────────────────────────────┐
│ Vacancy details are sent for inclusion in
│ internal vacancy bulletin and advertised
│ externally (ie press, job centres, etc)  │
└─────────────────────────────────────┘
                    ▼
┌─────────────────────────────────────┐
│ Application packs issued within 48 hours
│            of request                │
└─────────────────────────────────────┘
                    ▼
```

┌─────────────────────────────────────┐   ┌─────────────────────────────────┐
│ Applications received from candidates on │──► │ Inside Track applicant meets the │
│ the Inside Track that meet the shortlisting │ │ criteria and is offered the post │
│   criteria should be interviewed │   └─────────────────────────────────┘

┌─────────────────────────────────────┐   ┌─────────────────────────────────┐
│   │   │ No applicant is suitable for the │
│ Applications received and panel shortlist │──► │ post – re-examine the job descrip-│
│ against person specification criteria │   │ tion, person specification and   │
└─────────────────────────────────────┘   │ advert, and then re-advertise   │
                    ▼   └─────────────────────────────────┘

┌─────────────────────────────────────┐   ┌─────────────────────────────────┐
│ Shortlisted applicants are invited to │   │ Applications from candidates   │
│ attend for interview. Verification of *Per-* │──► │ not shortlisted are retained for │
│ *mission to Work in the UK* form sent to can- │ │ four months, together with indi- │
│ didates. References taken up   │   │ vidual shortlisting proformas and│
└─────────────────────────────────────┘   │ reasons for not shortlisting form│
                    ▼   └─────────────────────────────────┘

┌─────────────────────────────────────┐
│ Interviews take place. Applicants are │
│ assessed against the person specification
│ criteria. Verification of *Permission to Work*
│ *in the UK* form is checked by appointing
│   manager   │
└─────────────────────────────────────┘
                    ▼

┌─────────────────────────────────────┐   ┌─────────────────────────────────┐
│ Applicant meets the person specification │──► │ No applicant meets the person   │
└─────────────────────────────────────┘   │ specification. Re-examine the   │
                    ▼   │ vacancy details and re-advertise │
                                                └─────────────────────────────────┘
┌─────────────────────────────────────┐
│ Offer is made, subject to references satis-
│ factory to Scope, medical clearance,
│ Immigration and police checks where
│ applicable. Written offer sent by appoint-
│ ing manager and/or start date is estab-
│ lished and a Request for Contract form is
│   sent to HR   │
└─────────────────────────────────────┘
                    ▼
┌─────────────────────────────────────┐
│ Unsuccessful interview candidates are │
│   notified.   │
└─────────────────────────────────────┘

Appendix 3: BBC

The following is extracted from the BBC's *Information for Staff Handbook*, reproduced with kind permission of the BBC.

Conditions of service

The Corporate framework on conditions of service consists of core conditions which apply to all staff across the BBC, together with a code of practice within which each Directorate works.

Core conditions

Conditions which apply to all staff:

- for hours staff, basic working time based on an average of 40 hours/week (including meals)
- for days staff, an underlying requirement to work a minimum of 40 hours/week (including meals)
- annual leave entitlement of five weeks (plus public holidays and an extra day at Christmas), plus additional leave for staff with longer service
- unpredictability allowances
- protected days off.

In addition to these, there are other employment provisions which apply to all staff, eg

- sick pay scheme
- maternity and parental support benefits
- the BBC pension scheme/group personal pension plan
- redundancy and early retirement benefits
- accident and death in service benefits
- appeals and grievance procedures
- disciplinary procedures
- severance pay
- special leave arrangements; and
- the BBC's employment policies in equal opportunities, occupational health and safety

all of which are outlined in this handbook.

Sick absence

If you are ill and not able to attend for work you must advise your manager as soon as possible. You must also provide whatever medical certificates are required and keep the BBC informed about your availability for work. There is no entitlement to paid sick absence, which is granted at the discretion of the BBC. However, provided you satisfy the requirements set out in the BBC booklet 'Sick Absence and Statutory Sick Pay' you can expect to be granted paid sick absence as follows:

- less than two years' continuous service – up to four weeks for each illness, and an aggregate of 13 weeks;

- two years' or more continuous service – up to
  eight weeks for each illness and an aggregate of 26
  weeks in any period of two years' service
  calculated up to 31 December following the date
  of going sick.

During sick absence you are not expected to do anything which is inconsistent with being unfit for your BBC duties or which delays your return to work. To work for another employer without prior agreement or to take part in inappropriate social or sporting activities is regarded as a serious breach of discipline.

If you have a period of sick absence in excess of three months, your annual leave entitlement may be reduced pro rata, in the light of your particular circumstances.

Redundancy and redeployment

The BBC seeks to safeguard employment for all its staff. At the same time it is a dynamic organisation and changes do occur. New methods of working are regularly being introduced and departments are re-organised. This has an effect on the work which needs to be done and the numbers and categories of staff required. When this occurs and fewer people are needed for work of a particular kind some staff may become redundant. In co-operation with the member of staff affected every effort is made to find alternative employment within the BBC; initially within the same Directorate, but also in any other area where suitable opportunity may exist. When no alternative employment is available, the BBC Job Shop helps individuals to look for employment outside the BBC.

INSTITUTE OF PERSONNEL
AND DEVELOPMENT

Customer Satisfaction Survey

We would be grateful if you could spend a few minutes answering these questions and return the postcard to IPD. Please use a black pen to answer. **If you would like to receive a free IPD pen, please include your name and address.**

....

1. Title of book ....

2. Date of purchase: month ....   year ....

3. How did you buy this book?
   ☐ Bookshop   ☐ Mail order   ☐ Exhibition

4. If ordered by mail, how long did it take to arrive:
   ☐ 1 week   ☐ 2 weeks   ☐ more than 2 weeks

5. Name of shop .... Town.. Country ....

6. Please grade the following according to their influence on your purchasing decision with 1 as least influential: (please tick)

	1	2	3	4	5
Title					
Publisher					
Author					
Price					
Subject					

7. On a scale of 1 to 5 (with 1 as poor & 5 as excellent) please give your impressions of the book in terms of: (please tick)

	1	2	3	4	5
Cover design					
Page design					
Paper/print quality					
Good value for money					

8. Did you find the book:
   Covers the subject in sufficient depth   ☐ Yes   ☐ No
   Useful for your work   ☐ Yes   ☐ No

9. Are you using this book to help:
   ☐ In your work   ☐ Personal study   ☐ Both   ☐ Other (please state) ....

Please complete if you are using this as part of a course

10. Name of academic institution...

11. Name of course you are following? ....

12. Did you find this book relevant to the syllabus? ☐ Yes ☐ No ☐ Don't know

Thank you!

To receive regular information about IPD books and resources call 0181 263 3387.
Any data or information provided to the IPD for the purposes of membership and other Institute activities will be processed by means of a computer database or otherwise. You may, from time to time, receive business information relevant to your work from the Institute and its other activities. If you do not wish to receive such information please write to the IPD, giving your full name, address and postcode. The Institute does not make its membership lists available to any outside organisation.

2

Publishing Department

Institute of Personnel and Development

IPD House

Camp Road

Wimbledon

London

SW19 4BR